THE CAVIAR SAVANT

100 FACTS ABOUT THIS RARE DELICACY AND WHAT EVERY CONNOISSEUR SHOULD KNOW

BY

PENNY D. NICHOLS

Copyright

First published by Parker Project Publishers 2023

Copyright © 2023 by Penny D. Nichols.

All rights reserved. No part of this publication may be reproduced, stored, or transmitted in any form or by any means, electronic, mechanical, photocopying, recording, scanning, or otherwise, without written permission from the publisher. It is illegal to copy this book, post it to a website, or distribute it by any other means without permission.

Penny D. Nichols asserts the moral right to be identified as the author of this work.

Penny D. Nichols has no responsibility for the persistence or accuracy of URLs for external or third-party Internet Websites referred to in this publication and does not guarantee that any content on such Websites is, or will remain, accurate or appropriate.

Designations used by companies to distinguish their products are often claimed as trademarks. All brand names and product names used in this book and on its cover are trade names, service marks, trademarks, and registered trademarks of their respective owners. The publishers and the book are not associated with any product or vendor mentioned in this book. None of the companies referenced within the text have endorsed the book.

First edition

This book was professionally typeset on Reedsy.

Find out more at reedsy.com

DEDICATION

Dedicated to Ronnie, Maxine, and Chuck

for the foundation.

To Veronica and Hannah

For the journey.

Table of contents

COPYRIGHT i
DEDICATION iii
TABLE OF CONTENTS iv
PREFACE v
HISTORICAL FACTS AND ISSUES WITH CAVIAR 1
TOP 5 VARIETIES OF CAVIAR 9
THE MARKET: TOP 10 EXPORTERS OF CAVIAR 13
TOP 10 COUNTRIES FOR CONSUMER CONSUMPTION PER CAPITA 17
CELEBRATING WITH CAVIAR - CULTURAL PREFERENCES 20
THE INCREDIBLE HEALTH BENEFITS OF CAVIAR 25
CAVIAR IN POP CULTURE "QUOTES" FROM CELEBRITIES 30
THE DARK SIDE 37
MUSINGS, RANTS, AND CONUNDRUMS 41
SPEAKING OF RESTAURANTS AND TRENDS 49
THE RECIPES, OF COURSE, ... 58
CONCLUSION 67
ABOUT THE AUTHOR 70

Preface

Welcome people to the world of the Caviar Savant – A world of Luxurious lifestyles: A-listers, MEGA-yachts, expensive Expensive, EXPENSIVE everything, everywhere and all at once. The one-percenters join the global elite who mingle with the "Page-6ers," who invite you to enter their world of luxurious opulence and complex intrigue of the highest order. Caviar – No other word lends itself to the same level of mystique – evoking dreams of finally Arriving with a capital A, achieving and exceeding one's hopes and beyond. Caviar - a word so emotional it represents the quasi-essential feelings behind life's milestone celebrations: honoring a valued mentor, a well-deserved promotion, as well as expressing love for family and friends with a gift so rare, so revered as to set the stage for a very bold Bond, James Bond moment.

We're talking about fish eggs on the other end of the spectrum. The sordid history of the lowly sturgeon from its prehistoric beginning to the table of czars reeking thoughts of sacrificed tragedy. With the

Russian-Ukrainian war raging, is Putin's regime aggression against Ukraine a ploy to recapture the waters of Russia's past that are now in Ukraine's spawning grounds? Is this war to reclaim the memories of a glorious Russia just the epitome of hubris for the ex-KGB operative? Is the market for traditional Caviar becoming the symbol of greed and global decadence? But I digress….

> Prepare yourself for your initiation to the "Members Only" club, where one is expected to know at least something about.
>
> **-Caviar.**

This book is intended as an insider's guide to the world of Caviar: its place as a luxury food product. Know how the market desecrates what Caviar is - and examine how it's morphed and commingled with non-caviar products. Its connotation in today's pop culture…. can you say, Kanye? - oh, so yesterday, today it's Ye - and so on……

Lastly, it's a compilation of Caviar recipes, facts, trends, musings, and a few conundrums to ponder in your ongoing knowledge and enjoyment.

01

Historical Facts and Issues with Caviar

1

From a historical perspective, you can't talk about Caviar until you identify its source. This rare delicacy is produced from the eggs of the Beluga Sturgeon fish, which has existed since the Triassic period more than 200 million years ago. This bottom feeder is essential because this species, which swam during the age of the dinosaurs, are facing extinction from over-fishing, climate change, human intervention, and environmental calamities.

The threats to their very survival come from a myriad of obstacles besides natural causes; they must also contend with poaching, global over-fishing, habitat degradation of spawning grounds, unscrupulous fish roe vendors, unsafe aqua-farming practices in addition to being collateral damage in ongoing criminal activities of human trafficking and political neglect, especially in regulatory compliance. In 2005 the U.S. Fish and Wildlife Service banned the import of all Beluga products from the Caspian Sea, curtailing its demise. More about the Sturgeon later…

The Greek philosopher Aristotle first documented the food called Caviar in the 4th century B.C. Brought by

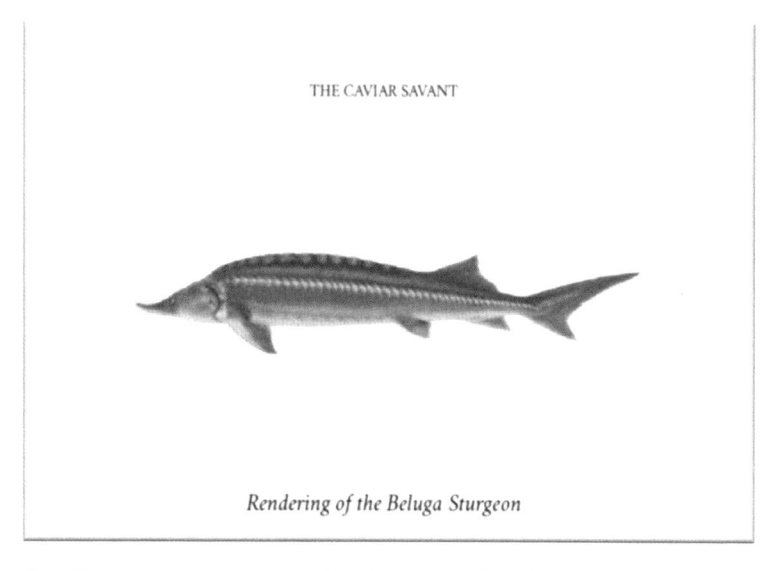

THE CAVIAR SAVANT

Rendering of the Beluga Sturgeon

the Persians to courtly feasts, the locals caught the sturgeon in the Caspian Sea. They lightly salted the unfertilized eggs of the female from the salt mined nearby, improving the flavor and preserving the roe for transport. It was used as a spread like we use butter today.

The Greeks traded with the Russians of the region, and soon Caviar appeared on the table of the czars of the Russian court.

The Russian czars were so enamored with Caviar that the taste for it gradually spread to the British Court - who quickly seized the spawning waters of the land they controlled and decreed the bounty for themselves. Known as "the Royal fish," the sturgeon population spawning grounds in the U.K. are still considered tourist attractions and, if taken, are the personal property of the monarchy as a part of their "royal prerogative." As the taste for Caviar spread through Europe, the price rose, and the market grew. The more advanced salting and cooling process, originating from China, is given the context here because this increased the preservation quality and, thus, the marketability of Caviar for trade.

In Russia, Persia, and Europe, authentic Caviar, sometimes called the "Czar's caviar," consists only of unfertilized Sturgeon roe taken from a mature female. Beluga, considered the finest of the Sturgeon roes, competes in this category with Ossetra and Sevruga. Their roe ranges in color from large light gray pearls (Beluga), amber pearls (Ossetra), and medium size black pearls (Sevruga).

American sturgeon was first found in the Columbia and Delaware Rivers as the delicacy moved to the U.S. A German immigrant fostered the growing American Caviar industry. After that, the US became the largest exporter of Caviar to Europe. As the European taste preferred Russian Caviar, some of the American Caviar became repackaged and returned to America, relabeled as "Russian" Caviar at a higher price. Corruption in the grading and standardizing of this luxury food began as the supply and demand fluctuated. - even today, there is global standardization for marketing, but labeling violations and non-conformity for this product are difficult to detect, so compliance has not been universal - only the market forces and reputation of the producers themselves determine their value.

By the 1920s, Caviar's popularity grew along with America's middle class due to the "Black Gold," as it was called. Get-rich schemes lured people like the Alaskan gold rush and inspired those seeking wealth and fame. Upwardly mobile Americans began the tradition of celebrating special milestones with rare culinary delights: Chocolates, Shellfish, Fillets of beef and lamb, fine Brandy, and Caviar.

Not only for royalty any longer, "Hollywood" royalty and tycoon moguls became the new symbols of the American Dream…. The symbol of "Making it in America" was being embraced, and with it, the increased demand for Caviar.

Quietly, the underpinnings of the industry began to decay. While the sturgeon had been a resident of the seas and rivers for 200 million years, in less than 100 years, the Caviar industry is facing extinction. A female Surgeon doesn't produce eggs until after its 10th year and has a lifespan of 100 years. Only a minute percentage of sturgeons live their entire life cycle. Protesters of the wild sturgeons' struggles ramped up efforts for its salvation. Those voices were too weak and yet to be seen, perhaps too late. Although import and export bans have been in place for 18 years of this writing, their numbers in the wild are still dwindling dramatically.

Today's future of the Caviar industry as we know it has evolved; some say it's being expanded, while others say polluted by adding other fish roes. While a small segment still occupies the market - the Caviar term is being filtrated with niche products capitalizing off the Caviar mystic - these products are so-called "alternative caviar" for grading and standardization purposes. These alternatives include trout roe, salmon roe, other fish roe, vegan Caviar, and even powdered Caviar. Marketing products such as Facial Caviar are adding to the confusion, moving it from a luxury food product into the beauty and health niche. On a recent purchasing trip, it was a "Truffled Whitefish Caviar" product, and opening a fashion magazine to find a *Caviar* smart watch band – quite attractive. These non-caviar alternatives are marketed without much distinction to fill the void or scarcity of …. well…. traditional Caviar.

02

Top 5 Varieties of Caviar

2

There are currently 25 varieties of sturgeon making up the species. The following are considered the top 5 that produce the best Caviar available today.

Beluga caviar. Make no mistake, the Beluga sturgeon, a large, prehistoric fish that can reach 16 feet long at maturity and weigh nearly 3,000 pounds, produces the most coveted eggs. Found in the Caspian and the Black Sea, which is bordered by Russia, Azerbaijan, Iran, Kazakhstan, and Turkmenistan. This Caviar is rich, with just a hint of ocean saltiness, and ranges in color from pearl gray to very dark, the most precious of the best; it earns its "Black Gold" moniker. Even with import and export bans honored by governments worldwide, it faces extinction.

Kaluga caviar. The Kaluga is a large freshwater sturgeon whose Caviar is said to closely match the taste of Beluga caviar. Kaluga eggs are well-defined and smooth and have a lightly-salted buttery flavor. You will find this Caviar served at the finest restaurants and is the preferred garnish by chefs for its dark shine.

Osetra caviar. Slightly smaller than beluga caviar, osetra sturgeon eggs are golden to brown. The lighter the eggs, the older the fish, and the more expensive the osetra caviar. It has a naturally salty sea briny taste.

Sevruga caviar. This Caviar is from the eggs of three types of sturgeon from the Caspian Sea: Sevruga, Sterlet, and Siberian sturgeon. Eggs are small and gray and are one of the most in-demand types of Caviar with a distinct, bold flavor. Pablo Picasso insisted on Sevruga only when being served.

American Caviar. Derived from fish such as lake sturgeon, wild Atlantic sturgeon, and white sturgeon, it is found in the ocean as well as the rivers of its spawning ground. In the nineteenth century, the United States was a leading producer of Caviar. It has had a resurgence, and American Caviar has once again become popular with Americans.

03

The Market: Top 10 exporters of Caviar

3

Exporters of Caviar and the labeling of such take on new meanings when you look at the global market for luxury food products. Although Caviar has been one of the first on the list of luxury food product designation, currently, what is considered traditional Caviar is characterized as the following: roe from the internal egg masses of the wild sturgeon sourced from the Caspian Sea or the Mediterranean Black Sea, or as documented earlier as the Czars Caviar. Note that the market for traditional Caviar is ½ the size of the global caviar market, which includes caviar alternatives such as trout roe, salmon roe, vegan roe, synthetic powder, etc. The figures have been adjusted here to represent the Traditional Caviar market which is the focus of this book.

1. China
2. Italy
3. France
4. Germany
5. Belgium
6. Bulgaria
7. U.S.
8. Netherlands
9. Israel
10. Iran

ALGERIEN
Tamanrasset
LIBYEN
Murzuk
Tripolis
Bengasi
Kairo
ÄGYPTEN
Assuan
Al Jauf
El Jawf
TÜRKEI
MALTA
NIGER
TSCHAD
SUDAN
Khartum
Nyala
ERITREA
ÄTHIOPIEN
UGANDA
KENIA
SAHARA
AFRIKA

04

Top 10 countries for Consumer Consumption per Capita

4

It's no wonder that European countries rank as the top consumers of Caviar. Notice all the countries reside in the northern hemisphere where the Sturgeons spawning grounds are located. Considering its history and origin, it is still a staple of celebratory occasions for a luxury food product. The Southern Hemisphere has its luxury food products as well, but Caviar is opening up the market to the uber-rich in the southern hemisphere, with Uruguay as a competing source

1. France
2. Italy
3. Germany
4. Belgium
5. Bulgaria
6. US
7. Canada
8. Japan
9. Spain
10. Iran

05

Celebrating with Caviar - cultural preferences

5

Traditional Caviar and Caviar Alternatives - Can you see the difference?

Countries and regions have integrated their celebratory customs, including Caviar, as a rare and unforgettable delight. The French, the largest consumer of Caviar per capita, enjoy their Caviar served neat in a bowl of crystal or silver set upon cooling ice to keep it fresh and eaten with small Mother-of-pearl spoons accompanied by a sparkling glass of champagne.

The Russians who have been enamored of Caviar for centuries typically enjoy Beluga or Sevruga on top of blinis, buckwheat pancakes topped with a dollop of creme fraiche and garnished with just a smidgen of dill to freshen the palate. The drink of choice is almost always vodka; shots served frozen to a syrupy consistency and perhaps garnished with a few pink peppercorns for spark.

In Italy, the best-known style of serving Caviar is as a garnish with freshly cooked pasta or omelet and served with an Italian Prosecco.

Japan enjoys Caviar as an addition to a sashimi selection, but it is not served in the tin. It is seasonally served or thawed from frozen with a marinade of soy sauce to heighten the flavor. Most times, Caviar is used as a garnish for other dishes. Scooped carefully with chopsticks and served with cold, unfiltered Sake.

In Denmark, Caviar is a treat for New Year's Eve and is served at midnight to celebrate the joys of the coming year.

In America, Caviar has shifted from an elegant celebratory luxury on special occasions to being "cool." It's more of a destination with the upwardly mobile set and downplays its historical significance, which is the foundation of its mystique. Now it's touted for its dietary health benefits and its cache as a symbol of health and wealth. Be it the trend in the nuanced fashion world of the see-and-be-seen crowd with bottle service. Caviar has become its own iteration of the "cool" caviar mystique. However, if you D.O. eat Caviar, take your time and do not chew it but allow the pearls to settle on your tongue and melt gradually - then smoosh the gelatinous spoonful against the roof of your mouth. Universally, the best Caviar is usually served unadorned by the ever-loving, Mother-of-pearl spoonful.

Osetra Amber pearls

06

The incredible health benefits of Caviar

6

Minerals

Amounts Per Selected Serving		%DV
Calcium	44.0 mg	4%
Iron	1.9 mg	11%
Magnesium	48.0 mg	12%
Phosphorus	57.0 mg	6%
Potassium	29.0 mg	1%
Sodium	240 mg	10%
Zinc	0.2 mg	1%
Copper	0.0 mg	1%
Manganese	0.0 mg	0%
Selenium	10.5 mcg	15%
Fluoride	~	

Who knew? Caviar could be our next Superfood, after all. All the nutrients, zero sugar, and rich in omega fats. Caviar is usually sold in small quantities in the 1-ounce or 30-gram tins. It's Kosher, Keto, and Its concentrated eggs are loaded with all the good stuff.

Let's look at the nutritional value of 1 ounce of Caviar:

- Minerals include Calcium, Iron, Phosphorus, Magnesium, and Selenium
- Vitamins include: A, B1, B2, B3, B5, B6, B7, B9, D, K

These vitamins help break down the carbohydrates and fats we consume daily, converting them to energy. Necessary for developing our bodies' cellular structure, red blood cells, and normal nerve function. Most of us receive enough vitamin B through our food, but deficiencies occasionally occur.

Symptoms of vitamin B deficiency include:

- Anemia.
- Confusion.
- Depression.
- Dry Skin.
- Skin rashes.
- Fatigue.
- Numbness.

Individuals at risk of developing a vitamin B deficiency include older adults, breastfeeding women, and pregnant women. For those label junkies out there...

1 ounce of Caviar also contains

- 5g Total Fat.
- 1g Saturated Fat.
- 7 g Protein.
- 71 Calories.
- 0g Sugar.
- g Fiber.
- 1 Carbohydrate.
- Omega 3 Fatty Acid.

- Amino Acids.
- Choline.

So, it is written that there's a possibility that Caviar can improve overall mood, stabilize hormone levels and improve blood flow. Caviar can boost one's sex drive and thus is a preventative measure against cardiovascular disease. Try asking your primary physician to write a script for your next order of Caviar. Skim for Caviar on the menus at the most luxurious Spas worldwide as the health benefits are being touted as the latest trend - how could that be bad?

1 ounce Beluga Caviar - (not to scale)

07

Caviar in Pop Culture "Quotes" from celebrities

7

The difference between the American version of "Live Aid" and the British one - in England, if you wanted a cup of tea, you made it yourself. If you wanted a sandwich, you brought it. In typical American style, at the American concert, there were laminated tour passes backstage and champagne and Caviar.

By Phil Collins, Singer, and Rock Star of Genesis.

Fame is like Caviar. You know it's well to have Caviar, but not when you have it every meal.

By Marilyn Monroe, Actress, Celebrity icon.

Some people want champagne and Caviar when they should have a beer and hot dogs.

By Dwight D Eisenhower, President of the United States.

Do the things you fear the most. Courage is an acquired taste, like Caviar.

By Erica Jong. Author, Feminist

For me, true luxury can include Caviar or a day with no meetings, appointments, or schedule.

By Michael Kors, a Fashion designer.

French fries. I love them. Some people are chocolate and sweets people. I love French fries, that, and Caviar.

> By Cameron Diaz, Actress.

My favorite snack is Caviar.
> By Kelsey Grammer. T.V. Actor

I lived through the garbage. I might as well dine on the Caviar.
> By Beverly Sills, Opera Soprano

Wit ought to be glorious like Caviar, not spread about like marmalade.
> By Noel Coward, Author, and Playwright.

I'm Russian; I'm into men, diamonds, and Caviar
> By Irina Shayk, Fashion Model.

God didn't bless me with success so I could just eat Caviar all-day

By Kathy Lee Gifford, a T.V. Personality.

All of a sudden discovered that I was allergic to Caviar. It was the perfect metaphor for my life. When I could only afford lousy Caviar, I could undoubtedly eat it.

By Larry David. Actor, Screenwriter, and Comedian

I should be soaring away with my head tilted slightly towards the gods, feeding on the Caviar of Shakespeare. An actor must ACT.

By Laurence Olivier, Actor and Knight.

Working with Albert Brooks was the most fun I ever had on a movie. He's the Caviar of comedy. I mean, nobody's funnier... Nobody is more intelligent than Albert Brooks.

By Sharon Stone, Actress.

Caviar: It's like being kissed by a lusty Mermaid

By Niles Crane (T.V. show Frasier).

Joanna: "What is the gelatinous muck? When I tell you to pack staples, must I specify that you are to stock good Caviar and not this $1.99 fish bait?"

Andrew: "Yes, madam."

Joanna: "Caviar should be round and hard and of adequate size - and should burst in your mouth at precisely the right moment."

By Joanna Staten, Goldie Hawn's' character in the 1987 movie, Overboard, to Andrew, played by Roddy McDowall.

A Caviar Savant differs from the Caviar Snob in one very crucial aspect; a Caviar Savant is playful and never takes one's self too seriously -

By Penny D. Nichols, The Caviar Savant

The Caviar Snob - Not Penny D. Nichols

08

The Dark Side

8

The enjoyment of a rare delicacy like Caviar comes with a price. The true cost overshadows what we, as consumers pay in currency. The world can do better. By better, I mean better than past generations at making our environment a safer, more enjoyable, and more ethical planet. 25 species are remaining of sturgeon from the Acienseridae family -and all are on the Critically Endangered species list. Taking a deeper dive into uncharted waters, for those unfamiliar with the term critically endangered, it deems a species at risk of extinction within 20 years to be characterized as such. No other entire species on earth currently faces this ultimate threat. Habitat degradation of spawning waters, dam constructions, dredging, and housing encroachments have blocked essential migratory routes, and illegal poaching has not subsided. It has been documented, and analysts concur that most of the movement of trade in some European countries this past Christmas season was passing through illegal channels of distribution.

The Caviar market for traditional Caviar is expected to grow to $1.15 billion with projections through 2027, almost 9% per year. With advances in aquaculture, farming sturgeon has surpassed nature's ability to provide the necessary sturgeons in the wild. The critically endangered species has already lost two of their ilk in the last five years: the Chinese Paddlefish and the Yangtze Sturgeon - now extinct.

Contact the World Wildlife Fund to see how you can help.

World Wildlife Fund

US Headquarters 1250 24th Street, N.W.

Washington DC 20090-1193

1-800-960-0993

https://www.worldwildlife.org

World Wildlife Fund, Inc. is a nonprofit, tax-exempt charitable organization (tax I.D. number) (52-169338/) under section 501(c)(3)

09

Musings, Rants, and Conundrums

9

The female sturgeon doesn't lay her first eggs until maturity, approx. 12-18 years, much like humans' age of maturity. The visionary knows that the initial investment may be a decade away from the payout. The saying goes Time is Money. Sturgeons can live to be 100 and produce eggs once into maturity.

2.

The most expensive Caviar in the world comes from the eggs of the Albino Osetra Sturgeon "Almas" in the south Caspian Sea and is unequivocally deemed the rarest of the rare, the most prized of the prized. There exists a family of sturgeon that are between 60-100 years old and produce light golden white iridescent pearls. When last priced, one ounce was approximately $1,000. It's sold by the kilogram at $34,700. If available. This Caviar is rich and mildly salty with nutty and buttery notes. Put this one on your bucket list while it exists.

The Almas Iridescent white pearls

3.

The caviar alternatives have grown to be more than 65% of the total caviar market. As a caviar savant, I know that lurking on the sidelines is emerging an even more expensive product than the Almas caviar.

There is a marketing trend to capitalize on the "gold" caviar powder nomenclature. Caviar is dehydrated, and ground to dust, and 24-karat gold dust is mixed to make a culinary product used in high-end restaurants and catering and is finding its way into the Luxury Food Lane.

Also, another type of "gold" caviar is the bi-product of the selected caviar pearls that are deemed sub-par for packing but are pressed into blocks with a dusting of 24-karat gold dust, another caviar alternative—waste not-want not. Savants, unless you know how to source Caviar and navigate its pitfalls, purchasing from people you know and brands you trust in the Luxury food marketplace is always best. The "Gold" caviar internet hype is catching well-meaning people in its web of deceit. Don't be a victim and report unethical practices if you see them to protect this rare commodity and your community.

Food and Drug Administration
10920993 03 New Hampshire Ave,
Silver Springs, MD 20993
1-888-463-6332

4.

Historically, George Washington was known to fish for sturgeon on the banks of the Potomac River as a favorite pastime.

5.

In his book The Great Gatsby, F. Scott Fitzgerald said about the 1920s that Champagne and Caviar parties were replacing seated dinner parties and becoming the "height of affection" and avoided them if possible.

6.

The restaurant Caviar Kaspia in Paris (also, as of the writing, in St. Tropez, San Paulo, London, NYC, and Los Angeles) has been known since opening the Paris location in 1927 for sourcing only from reputable and quality suppliers. It attracts a global community of A-listers from all industries and governments. Keeping Up with the Kardashians featured an episode filmed there during Paris fashion week.... More on Caviar Kaspia....

7.

Sturgeon are found mainly in the Northern Hemisphere and live in oceans but spawn on the banks of freshwater rivers and estuaries. The word Caviar is believed to come from the Greek word for eggs and the Persian Khav-yar (English translation meaning Cake of Power)

8.

Malossol is a Russian term meaning "Little salt," and some caviar is labeled as such. This is preferred by some but not all - caviar savants of the world, you be the judge.

9.

Caviar, with its alternative products, maintains a certain equilibrium between demand and market supply. What was once the rarest symbol of sophistication and wealth; is now readily available by new means of logistics and delivery right to your door. The home delivery startup darling "Caviar" was recently acquired by DoorDash.

10.

Know that No caviar on earth is Red. The gorgeous giant roe of salmon qualifies as the king of the alternate caviar class, but it is not from the eggs of a Sturgeon and, therefore, is not Caviar. Spread the word.

11.

Yes, in Virginia, there is a National Caviar Day. It's July 18th, and what better time to try out a new Caviar offering at a local restaurant with the other Savants in the know?

12.

With everything godly within me - the next chapter is about the ideal places to enjoy a caviar service worthy of the indulgent experience. With all the strength I could muster, I removed the Iconic Russian Tea Room in NYC from the list. Its memories will remain intact, and don't hate me because I'm being honest. Like Russia, its glorious past must rest with the ghosts of the czars and even Gorbachev. I refuse to step into the abyss and suggest it is anything else but unworthy of your consideration. That being said - this is not a political statement. Be aware Russians do not own the Russian Tea Room and, as a 95-year-old Manhattan relic - is speaking out against the current communist dictatorship and has posted the following statement " Just as the founders, Soviet defectors who were displaced by the revolution, stand against Russian President Vladimir Putin and with the people of Ukraine."

As a restaurant, however, decay is decay, making my soul ache. I pray it will soon be back and Ukraine liberated.

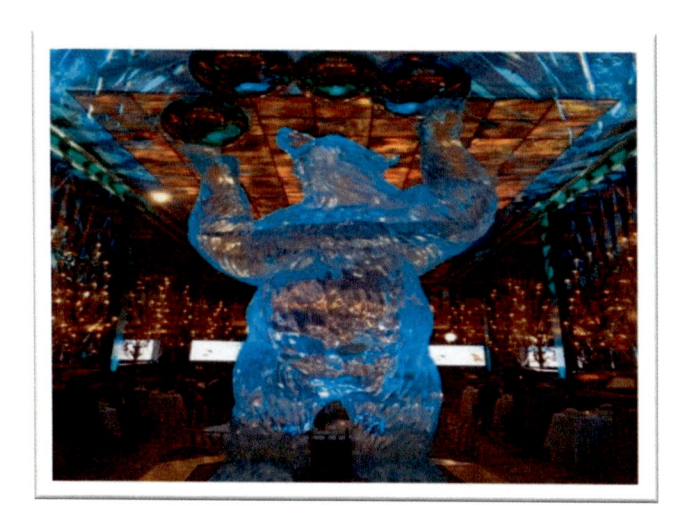

The Russian Tea Room

10

Speaking of restaurants and trends

10

It's Bucket List time. Although it's hard to narrow the list of the best global restaurants to splurge on for the caviar experience if you're adding to your bucket list, here are seven that will not disappoint:

The Snow Lodge (pop-up bar) - Aspen

There is a culinary trend that might embed itself into my heart. The pop-up caviar bar? Yes Please. When in Aspen, Ski to The Snow Lodge's tent at St. Regis for a glass of bubbly - Nicolas Feuillatte champagne and pair it with a "caviar bump" for the perfect après ski moment.

The Snow Lodge 315 Dean St.
Aspen, CO 81611
Tel -(970) 429-9581

Caviar Kaspian - Paris

They have committed since 1927 to have Caviar always on the menu following the traditional Russian caviar format. Their pre-revolutionary decor and vast caviar selection ensure they meet and exceed customers' preferences. You can have Caviar as a garnish or as much as the law allows served your way. The Iconic turquoise blue linens and minaret-shaped ashtrays still adorn the table setting. The crystal seal once belonging to Czar Nicolas II still evokes visions of the Russian Court. (Note their global expansion as they recently soft-opened their

Manhattan location. St. Tropez, Sao Paulo, London, Dubai, and Los Angeles) all the world's their oyster.

Recommended dish: Pomme de Terre Caviar Imperial 50 Grs, Jus de Fruits

Caviar Kaspian
17 Place de la Madeleine, Paris 75008
Tel: 33 1 42 65 33 32
www.caviarkaspia.com

Disfrutar- Barcelona

The best restaurant in Barcelona with its two Michelin stars always, and I always mean over-delivers. Breaking new ground as a standout since 2014, their food porn presentations are true art. From the garnish of frozen egg yolk with transparent almond to their 28-course "Disfrutar Festival" with their bold flavors and courageous offerings, they still manage to serve Caviar in inventive machinations - but somehow make them feel classic. Bucket list? Oh yes.

Disfrutar

Carrer de Villarroel, 163 Barcelona Spain 08036
Tel: (+23) 933-48-68-96
www.disfrutarbarcelona.com for reservations

Amuse at Disfrutar

Caprice - Hong Kong

French - Vegetarian-friendly

I'm not usually a fan of overpriced hotel restaurants; although always lovely, they are not memorable, and the experience seems sterile. Not so with Caprice. This 6-Star rated Four Seasons hotel, with its 3-star

Michelin standout, deserves all the accolades in a city known for exquisite food and attention to detail. The superior service and stunning harbor views will win any savant over, but let us not forget this is a caviar review. China, the leading exporter of Caviar, knows how to serve and present this delicacy. Their Caviar menu is varied with the czars' traditional presentations. It can be ordered solo or as one course in the Chef's Signature Tasting Menu, or the Menu Collection allows you to select Caviar with the other food selections. Cost-wise - be prepared. The upgrades in Caviar will cost you dearly, upwards of $650. per person to make substitutions. The addition of the caviar service and other exquisite selections makes this an unforgettable experience.

Caprice

Four Season Hotel
8 Finance Street Central Hong Kong
Tel: +(852) 3196-8882
www.fourseasons.com

When you find yourself in Hong Kong, why not also try one of their famous Caviar Bars: Mandarin Grill

& Bar, 1 Michelin Star - order the Caviar Service at the bar.

"I'll have the Caviar service, please, and may I also mortgage my house – we are in the financial district – right?"

- Penny D. Nichols

Caprice and Caviar Carpaccio

HUSO - NYC

You can buy the HUSO Caviar at their retail store before leaving for $830 -but have lunch or dinner there first. Located behind the curtain of the Boutique, enter a world of artfully presented extravagance with the top Chef winner in 2019. You can indulge in their artfully crafted menu or enjoy champagne with Caviar to your heart's content. Unlike the Wizard of O.Z., pay attention to what's behind the curtain at HUSO.

HUSO – NYC

1067 Madison Ave. NYC, NY 10028
Tel (212) 288-0850
www.huso@husony.com

Petrossian Restaurant & Boutique - Los Angeles Opened in 2001, this perfect marriage of California casual and Caviar chic was a winning combination. Still, family owned and specializes in Caviar. Specifically, California sourced and only open to 5 pm as of late. Check hours and availability before you go. A victim of the pandemic saw them down but not out. Although they have scaled back on hours, their quality of service remains intact. They made it through the pandemic without selling out. A true American Born haven with a beautiful patio to optimize the beautiful weather of California - indeed, the Golden State. Speaking of Golden - mosey on over to the Boutique after lunch, where you can buy the tins of Petrossian Caviar to take home. This family-owned restaurant is a bargain for its artful food presentations and ability to make every customer feel like family. The unpretentious chic California vibe will have you coming back again and again. Why not begin the adventure with the Beluga Martini - (Thank you for asking) Beluga vodka with olives stuffed with Caviar – and served sparkling ice cold? It's casual there, so go for the $65: brunch or the Ocetra Service. Sit outdoors on the patio in trendy West Hollywood; perhaps you'll be discovered.

Petrossian Restaurant & Boutique
321 North Robertson Blvd.
West Hollywood, CA 90048
Tel: 310-271-6300
wehoassistant@petrossian.com

11

The Recipes, of course,

11

Recipes to host at home

Caviar demands center stage when it's presented at banquets and restaurants. The presentation and the garnishes are all flawless. Even when indulging alone, serve it cold and partake by the spoonful.

Buckwheat Blinis with Caviar- Recipe of the Czar's

INGREDIENTS

- 2/3 cup all-purpose flour
- ½ Tbsp sugar
- 1 Tbsp active dry yeast
- 1 cup milk, warmed to 98°F 1/2 cup buckwheat flour
- 1 tsp salt
- One large egg, separated at room temperature
- 2 Tbsp heavy cream
- ¼ cup clarified butter melted 1 Tbsp chives, chopped
- 1 Tbsp red onion, finely diced 1 Tsp crème fraiche
- 1 oz choice of Osetra Caviar, Kaluga, Huso Huso, or Beluga

DIRECTIONS:

In a large bowl, sift flour, salt, and sugar. Make a well in the center and pour the lukewarm milk and yeast, whisking until the batter is smooth. Cover the batter with a damp towel and let the batter rise for about an hour. Stir the melted butter into the batter, and lastly, stir in the beaten egg yolk. In a separate bowl, whisk the egg white until stiff but not dry. Fold the whisked egg white into the batter. Cover the bowl again and let the batter stand for 20 minutes; Pan-fry the blini by heating a large skillet over medium heat. Add a tablespoon of butter and drop a spoonful dollop into the Pan; Cook until bubbles form, about 1 minute. Flip over and cook approx. 30-45 additional seconds. Repeat the frying process keeping the finished blinis warm for serving.

Serve with an assorted garnish of finely diced red onion, 1 tsp chopped chives, 1 tsp creme fraiche, chopped egg white, and separate chopped egg yolk if desired.

Serve in a caviar bowl over ice to keep it cold. Mother-of-pearl spoons add a final delicate touch to your presentation.

Citrus Creme Fraiche

Add 1 cup of creme fraiche, ½ cup lemon zest, and ½ cup orange zest. Stir in one tbs. of lemon juice and garnish with pomegranate arils. Serve with Caviar during the summer months.

Sweet Potato Pancakes with Caviar

INGREDIENTS:

- 1½ cups Shredded Sweet Potato or Japanese Yam
- 2 tbsp all-purpose flour
- ½ cup chopped onion
- ½ cup nutritional yeast
- Two eggs at room temperature
- 1 Tbsp Kosher salt

DIRECTIONS:

Mix all ingredients in a large bowl and refrigerate for 20 mins. Fry in a skillet with ½ cup olive oil and 1 tbsp butter over medium heat. Fry each side until the edges turn golden brown approx. Six minutes then flip over and fry for another minute. Remove and serve hot with creme fraiche and finish with two tbsp of Caviar on top.

Hannah's Appetizer - Easy way to serve in a hurry

On a large tray, lay a single layer of Kettle style potato chips (I like ones with ridges as an option), add a small amount of creme fraiche and a dollop of Caviar with a bit of fresh dill and serve, Caviar has long paired with potatoes, and this is a quick way to get the crunch and the burst of the Caviar pearls in an easy appetizer. Serve with champagne or, in Texas, a Ranch Water cocktail with Lalo tequila and lime wedge.

Caviar for Breakfast - eggs, cheese, and caviar sandwich

Serve creamy scrambled or omelet folded with shredded young Gruyere. Top eggs with a spoonful of Caviar and dill

Or

Hard boil eggs for 12 mins, drain water, and chill for 20 mins. Cut in half and top with sour cream and Caviar (chopped red onion and capers optional)

Or

Serve a caviar sandwich: Black bread sliced thin, spread with unsalted butter and thinly sliced cucumber. Spread with two tablespoons of Caviar. (Red onion and fresh dill optional)

Cotton Candy Caviar Coupe
For a whimsical dessert fit for a king

Select a couple of champagne crystals and fill it to overflow with cotton candy about the size of a fist. Work quickly and add a spoonful of golden osetra. (Well drained). Serve immediately as the cotton candy will degrade once the Caviar touches - eat with your hands by removing and putting it all in your mouth, allowing the flavors to meld—an incredible sensation for the senses and oh-so-fun.

Compliments of Penny D. Nichols

Caviar Sea Board

You are trending lately with Caviar and adding Caviar alternatives. Not for the true savant, but fun to dabble in the fad. Add your favorite seafood to a board with garnishes of fresh cucumbers, other roes, and creme fraiche mixed with edible flowers. Make it your own, and add seasoned seaweed sheets (nori) for texture and color.

Conclusion

When my daughter, Hannah turned 12; she became a dedicated vegetarian. Now a married adult with unbelievably spoiled pets (Just kidding, Karat, Lucy, and Josephine), she still consumes a plant-based diet – after all, "It's not nice to eat our animal friends." An exception arose this year with her gentle introduction to "Caviar." She has struggled with the ethics of harvesting the sturgeon to obtain the eggs and cannot condone the practice. With the advent of aquaculture, while those methods have improved the lot of the sturgeon – when done correctly, she can see a future that could save the specie. Sturgeon's life parallels humans' age, maturity, and lifespan. However, they have been a species for 200 million years. To humans' blink-of-an-eye stay on earth, they could become extinct in the wild. It is indeed a problem for some caviar lovers.

We have enjoyed our journey of exploring Caviar service together. We are working to systematically reduce our carbon footprint and mitigate some habitat degradation (starting with my patio) to justify and continue our enjoyment of this rare, delicate, luxurious, and extravagant indulgence – **Caviar**.

I sincerely wish that **The Caviar Savant** and your appreciation of this subject have given you some knowledge and enjoyment. My one favor is to ask you to please submit an honest review of this book to Amazon.com.

I appreciate your patronage, and may all your Caviar dreams come true.

Penny D. Nichols

(10% of the proceeds of this book will be donated to the World Wildlife Fund to contribute to the betterment of mother earth and the preservation of all endangered species)

Some of the notable U.S. caviar-producing aquafarms include Stolt Sea Farm, Sterling Caviar, and Marshallberg Farm.

About the Author

Penny D. Nichols - lover of Caviar, grateful for the sunshine, seeker of all good things, impertinent and possible-global tourist, mastermind, problem solver, MBA, Adjunct Professor, and so much more….